Baking
with
Grace

girl
OF THE
YEAR

Discover the recipe
for ooh-la-la!

by Trula Magruder

★ American Girl®

Published by American Girl Publishing
Copyright © 2015 American Girl

Questions or comments? Call 1-800-845-0005, visit **americangirl.com**, or write to Customer Service, American Girl, 8400 Fairway Place, Middleton, WI 53562-0497.

Printed in China
15 16 17 18 19 20 21 LEO 10 9 8 7 6 5 4 3 2 1

All American Girl marks, Grace™, Grace Thomas™, and Girl of the Year™ are trademarks of American Girl.

Editorial Development: Trula Magruder, Emily Osborn
Art Direction and Design: Gretchen Becker
Production: Jeannette Bailey, Judith Lary, Paula Moon, Kendra Schluter, Cynthia Stiles
Photography: Joe Hinrichs, Youa Thao
Craft Stylist: Trula Magruder, Emily Osborn
Set Stylist: Casey Hull, Kim Sphar
Doll Stylist: Jane Amini, Meghan Hurley, Julia Kinney
Illustrations: Casey Hull, Monika Roe

Stock Photography: pp. 39, 40—© istock.com/studiogstock; pp. 39, 40—© istock.com/marabird; pp. 33, 40—© istock.com/taice; pp. 19, 43—© istock.com/Yasonya; p. 33—© istock.com/Olya_Nikiparonak; pp. 8, 33—© istock.com/mimixformdesign

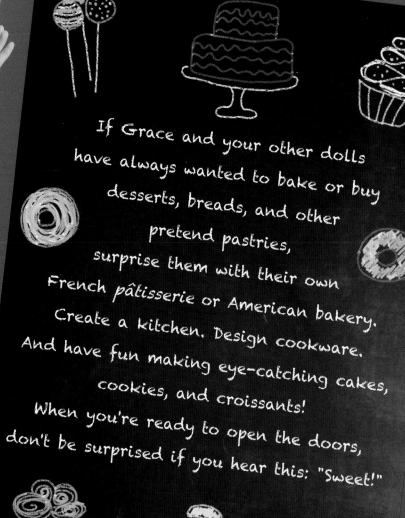

If Grace and your other dolls have always wanted to bake or buy desserts, breads, and other pretend pastries, surprise them with their own French *pâtisserie* or American bakery. Create a kitchen. Design cookware. And have fun making eye-catching cakes, cookies, and croissants! When you're ready to open the doors, don't be surprised if you hear this: "Sweet!"

Craft with Care

Keep Your Doll Safe

When creating doll crafts, remember that dyes from ribbons, felt, beads, cords, fabrics, fleece, and other supplies may bleed onto your doll or her clothes and leave permanent stains. To help prevent this, use lighter colors when possible, and check your doll often to make sure the colors aren't transferring to her body, her vinyl, or her clothes. And never get your doll wet! Water and heat greatly increase dye rub-off.

Get Help!

When you see this symbol  in the book, it means that you need an adult to help you with all or a part of the craft. ALWAYS ask for help before continuing.

Ask First

If a craft asks you to use an old item, such as a shirt, always ask an adult for permission before you use it. Your parent might still need the item, so check first.

Craft Smart

If a craft instruction says "cut," use scissors. If it says "glue," use craft glue or adhesive dots. And if it says "paint," use a nontoxic acrylic paint. Before you use these supplies, ask an adult to check them over—especially paints and glues. Some crafting supplies are not safe for kids.

Put Away Crafts and Supplies

When you're not using the crafts or art supplies, put them up high or store them away from little kids and pets. Toddlers and animals might eat your crafts, break them, or even hurt themselves when playing with them.

WARNING

Safely tuck your doll away while you create her bakery so that paint, glue, and other messy craft supplies don't get on your doll or her clothes. Make sure each project dries completely before you let your doll near it.

it Tools

our doll wants to make some "dough" at her
kery, she'll "knead" these sweet kit supplies.

corations
ded in the kit are some café labels to decorate vases, cups, jars, and
s for your doll. The provided signs and art can be used to decorate
nside of your doll's shop. Use the chalkboard paper to create fun
s, menus, or art of your own. Your doll can sit down at a café and
y the newspaper. Punch out the French flags and place them in your
s shop for additional flair.

od
the waffle cone paper to create ice cream cones. Punch out the
ghnuts for your doll's pastry shop. Use the sleeves to hold *baguettes*.
timer and recipe cards can help your doll create the perfect pastries.
 doll should use the oven mitt when handling hot things.

Chef's Gear

For a top chef, white is right.

Executive Coat

To dress your doll as a pastry chef, slip her into a long-sleeved white shirt or coat. If you don't have one, ask an adult if you can fold up the sleeves on a baby's white shirt. Press one of the kit's chef's coat-badge stickers to one side at the top of the coat.

Waist Apron

Cut an 8-inch square of white cotton fabric and two 8-inch white ribbon strips. Use fabric glue to attach the ribbon strips to the top corners of the fabric in back. Let dry. To tie on the apron, crisscross the straps around your doll's waist in back, and then tie them in a bow in front.

Chef's Scarf

To keep your chef looking cool—even in a warm kitchen—give her a neckerchief. To make one, cut white cotton fabric into a 9-by-9-by-13-inch triangle. Starting at the top point, roll up the scarf, and then tie it in a knot around your doll's neck.

Baker's Hat

Whether in America or France, a pastry chef needs a tiny *toque*.

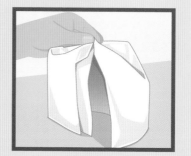

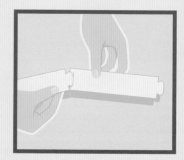

1. Fold a 20-by-20-inch sheet of **tissue paper** in half. Gather the folded edge and **tape** it into a tiny topknot.

2. Slot the 2 **hatbands** from your kit together at one end to make a single band. Tape them together on the back.

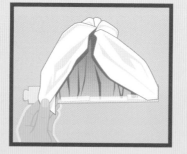

3. Turn the tissue paper inside out to hide the knot. Gather and tape the other edge along the length of the band.

4. Slot the ends of the band together, and tape them closed. Slip the toque on your doll's head and adjust the poof. *Voilà!*

BLUEBERRY MUFFINS

Standing Mixer

Make a mixer to create Grace's beautiful batters.

1. ✋⭐ Ask an adult to remove the batteries from an **old book light**. Stack and **glue** together 2 small **heart-shaped craft-wood pieces**.

2. Paint the wood with a **nontoxic acrylic paint** to match the light. Let dry. Slip the pointed end of the heart between the light's clip.

3. Pull out the kit's three **beater strips**. **Tape** each strip into a loop. Glue or tape the loops together as shown.

4. Cut a ½-inch piece off a **stirrer straw**. Glue one end of the straw to the top of the beater, and the other end to the light's bulb. Place a **doll's bowl** under the beater.

Making Muffins

Prepare blueberry muffins with Grace's secret ingredient—lemon!

Muffin Tin, Timer, and Recipe

Punch out the kit's kitchen timer and recipe card, and paint a plastic paint palette tray silver if you like. Gather other kitchen tools, such as a spatula and mixing bowl.

Blueberry Muffins

Fill a doll bowl with white nontoxic modeling clay. Use blue clay to make blueberries. Press a few on top of the batter. Pour glue over the remaining berries and let dry. For each finished muffin, open a small vending machine capsule, and place the domed-side up in a candy cup. Cover the dome with clay. Blend white, brown, and orange to get a baked-muffin-like color. Press on a few blue and purple clay balls for berries. Glue muffins onto a small plate.

Lemons

Shape yellow nontoxic modeling clay into lemons. Use a butter knife to cut a lemon in half. Make a narrow rim on the cut side with white clay for the pith. Glue lemons together in a doll bowl.

First Street Family Bakery

Design a tray of glazed doughnuts just as Grace's grandmother did.

Doughnuts

You can make bakery doughnuts in a variety of ways. Punch out the doughnuts from the kit. Or glue a few sheets of tan paper together, and cut circles with a small circle punch. Or cut out craft-foam circles with the same paper punch, and then glue colored paper to the doughnut for icing. Or make a craft-foam doughnut, and then use three-dimensional paint to frost it. Use a regular hole punch to make a center hole in the doughnuts.

Cinnamon Rolls

To make each roll, cut a ½-by-10-inch piece of tan felt and a ½-by-10-inch piece of dark brown felt. Stack the felt strips, and then roll them up. Run glue along the last inch, and wrap to close. Use a small rubber band to hold the felt in place until the glue dries. Frost the pastries with white three-dimensional paint. Let dry. Glue rolls to a doll-sized bakery tray or plate.

Bakery Trays

For each tray, cut a rectangle from silver adhesive craft foam. For a rim, cut a narrow strip of foam for each side. Cut a piece of wax paper to fit in the tray before adding the pastries.

Bon Voyage!

Design the bistro seating that Grace saw throughout Paris.

Parisian Dining Scene

Place your doll's table and chairs together to create a café scene. Use a white tablecloth for a fancier restaurant.

Table Essentials

Create a spot for dolls to catch up on their Parisian news. Remove the kit's newspaper, and fold it up for the table. Place some flowers in a small vase or jar.

Cocoa

If you have a doll-sized mug, serve hot cocoa. Cut a circle of brown craft foam just slightly larger than your doll's cup, and glue on white craft foam for whipped cream. Press the cocoa circle just inside the rim of the cup. Add a café label to the mug if you like.

La Pâtisserie

Every pastry Grace saw in the *pâtisserie,* or pastry shop, said, "Look at me!"

Pastry Cases and Counter

To make a pretty pastry case, look for decorative boxes from craft stores, or wrap cardboard boxes in pretty paper. Ask an adult to cut foam board for shelves. Make sure the shelves are tight enough to hold a little weight. Finish the shelf edges with decorative tape.

Pastries

Cakes: Decorate upside-down cupcake liners with stickers, beads, or glitter glue. To make chocolate curls, wrap brown-paper strips around a toothpick, and then slide the toothpick out.

Cookies: Use brown watercolor paint to "bake" small wooden pieces. Glue two of the same shapes together, and decorate with craft foam or paper. Glue the cookie assortment in a fancy array on a doll plate.

Fancy cakes: To make a selection of gourmet cakes, glue craft paper to different-sized craft boxes or tins, and decorate with scrapbook embellishments. Or glue a craft-foam circle on a wide ribbon roll. Or wrap a cardboard tube lid with pretty paper, and decorate it with punched paper shapes.

Gourmet Treats

Create the treats from *La Pâtisserie* that Grace photographed for her blog.

Macarons and *Éclairs*

For a *macaron*, punch out three same-sized small circles from craft foam, using a darker or lighter color for the center circle. Glue the pieces together—or use an adhesive craft foam to start with. For *éclairs*, cut out rounded rectangles from tan felt. Use brown paper for frosting. You can also glue on micro beads for sprinkles. Glue all treats to a doll plate.

Pies and *Tartes*

Use a large lid for a pie tin and a *tarte* tin. For a fruit filling, pour in beads, and squeeze glue over the top. For a top crust, weave strips of tan felt to cover the pie, glue the felt to the tin, and trim. Or cut a piece of tan felt to fit a lid, fold the felt in half, cut out a tiny heart, and glue the felt to the pie. For a chocolate cream or lemon meringue pie, fill the lid with brown or yellow three-dimensional paint. Let dry. Add polystyrene foam or tissue paper for whipped cream or meringue topping.

Crème Brûlée and *Flan*

For *crème brûlée*, cut a yellow craft-foam circle to fit inside a white lid. Color the foam with a brown crayon. For a *flan*, cover a round craft-box lid with yellow paper. Use a marker to color a caramel top. Use the marker to "spill" caramel onto a disposable plastic plate.

ies délicieuses

Breakfast Abroad

While in Paris, Grace relished the French pastries. Create a yummy breakfast for your doll!

Croissants

Cut a 2½-by-10-inch triangle from tan felt. Start at the base and tightly roll toward the point. Glue the tip to close. Bend the tips together for a minute or two to give the *croissant* its curved shape. Glue the *croissants* onto a doll plate or doll baking tin.

Apricot Jam

Use an old plastic paint pot for a jar. Wash the paint pot with soap and water, let dry, and then fill it with mini orange plastic beads. Squeeze glue on the beads to keep them in the pot. Attach the kit's jam labels to the lid and pot.

Orange Juice

Use scissors to trim an old, thin plastic glitter tube, or use a plastic cap. Wash, let dry, and then coat the inside with orange acrylic paint. Let dry. Add a fancy gold trim with duct tape if you like.

Strawberries

Shape strawberries from red and green nontoxic modeling clay. Poke the clay with a toothpick to add seeds. Let dry, and glue onto a doll plate.

Fresh Out of the Oven

Install ovens in the kitchen of your doll's bakery that look like *La Pâtisserie's* professional ones.

Convection Ovens

Find a cardboard box that's larger than four windowed bakery boxes. Cover the front and sides of the large box with silver wrapping paper. Glue or tape the bakery boxes to the larger box, leaving a gap between boxes so that the lids can open downward and there's room on one side for a panel. Add dials to the panel with 3-D scrapbook embellishments. If the bakery box lids won't stay closed, tape a rubber band inside the box next to the lid-closure slot, and then pull the rubber band through the slot so that it's outside the box. Across from the rubber band, punch a hole near the lid's edge. Slip a button shank (the back of the garment button) into the hole, and tape it in place inside. Slip the rubber band over the button to secure the lid.

Tray, Treats, and Oven Mitt

For a sheet pan, cut silver scrapbook paper into a large rectangle. To add a lip, fold in each side ¼ inch, unfold it, cut a slit in each corner, refold it, and glue closed. On the sheet pan, add wadded paper, biscuits cut from white nontoxic clay, and small flat wooden shapes. Use the kit's oven mitt to prevent burns!

La Boulangerie

Grace discovered French bakeries that sold only breads. Create a small *boulangerie*, or bakery, for your doll.

French Breads

Shape long, short, and round bread loaves from white, tan, or brown nontoxic clay. Use a butter knife or flat toothpick to make slits in the tops. Let dry. Brush the loaves with yellow, orange, red, and brown watercolor paint, and let dry. Scrape a piece of white nontoxic sidewalk chalk with a craft stick, and sprinkle the chalk on the bread for flour. Glue bread into bread bags, onto plates, or into baskets.

Bags and Baskets

Give your *boulangerie* European detail by storing your doll's breads in small baskets. Roll white paper into a mini bag to cover the bottom portion of the bread. Seal the bottom and side with tape. Or use one of the kit's bags.

Make Glace for Bastille Day

On this French holiday, dolls love ice cream. So include a *glace*, or ice cream, counter in your doll's *pâtisserie!*

Ice Cream Case and Holder

Use cake-pop gift boxes for a *glace* counter. Punch out square or round shapes from silver scrapbook paper, and cut different colors of craft foam in slightly larger shapes. Tape the foam to the back of the paper, and display the ice cream in the box. Use adhesive letters to write "*glace*" or "ice cream" on the counter, or use the kit's sign. For an ice cream holder, glue old glitter tubes to a lid. Leave enough room between tubes for the large scoops of ice cream!

Ice Cream Cones

Punch out the kit's cones, roll them up, and seal closed. Wad up tissue paper, and glue it inside the cone for ice cream.

Flag Fun

Show your doll's participation in Bastille Day by placing mini French flags on the counter. To make them, punch out the French flags from the kit, and then glue each one to a stirrer straw for your doll and her customers to wave or to use as decor.

Cookware Crazy

Grace adored Parisian cooking-supply stores—your doll will, too!

Cookware Cabinet

 Glue small wooden craft candlesticks to each corner of a large decorative box for legs. Paint the legs if you like. Ask an adult to cut foam-board shelves. Make sure the shelves fit tightly enough to hold a little weight.

Bowls

Gather different-sized bowls for the cookware cabinet. Use bottle caps, plastic capsules from toy vending machines, and *papier-mâché* craft lids. Paint the items to match if you like.

Bakeware and Cookware

Create baking pans from candy tins, craft boxes, lids, and plastic soap and candy molds. Paint them to match if you like. For a stove-top pan, wrap a craft stick in silver duct tape, and then glue it to the side of a round tin. Add a bead knob on top if you like.

Cake and Pie Displays

Add Parisian flair to your doll's pastry wares with cake stands, pie plates, and covers.

Covered Cake Plate

Use the round plastic container that cupcake liners come in to make a darling cake plate and cover. Glue a clear decorative bead in the center of the cover for a handle.

Cake Stand

Perch a cake on a fancy stand. To make one, attach a doll plate, a trimmed paper plate, or another flat object to an upside-down plastic drink glass or plastic cake pillar.

Pie Protector

To make a domed pie covering, look for a three-dimensional circle from plastic packaging, or use one half of a plastic craft ornament that separates into two halves.

Grand Opening

Leave a lasting impression of the bakery with these sweet ideas.

Meet and Greet

Expect a long line for the opening of your doll's bakery. Ask the pastry chef to greet customers—especially on the first day!

Bakery Boards

Use adhesive chalkboard paper to make a bakery board for outside your doll's bakery. Fold a piece of card stock into a tent, and attach the chalkboard paper. Write about the bakery's grand opening and the day's specials. Review "Chalkboard Writing" on page 30 to learn how to make the boards look professionally printed.

Themed Art

Create a look for your doll's bakery with wall art. Use the art in the kit; look for small painted art canvases of pastries, flowers, and other desserts; or paint your own! You can also match the colors in your doll's bakery with a solid, striped, or polka-dotted canvas. Let dry before placing the art on your doll's bakery walls.

Tiny Touches

Call attention to your doll's bakery with delicious or delightful details.

Bags and Boxes

Attach a pretty ribbon strap or baker's twine to your bakery boxes to make carrying easier. Your doll's customers will notice. If your doll runs out of boxes, resupply her with mini favor boxes—found at craft and wedding-supply stores. For bags, choose ones with handles so that dolls can slip them over their wrists.

Darling Details

Small niceties will go a long way at your doll's *pâtisserie* or bakery. Slip mini paper doilies under the cakes, keep flowers nearby, and pass out the bakery's business cards for special orders.

Number Dispenser

For days when your doll's bakery stays busy, make a number dispenser. First, ask an adult to remove the empty roll from a tape dispenser. Then cut a long paper strip the width the tape used to be, and wrap it on the roll. Slide the end of the paper roll through the dispenser, and attach one of the kit's number stickers. Fold a piece of cardboard or foam board into a counter tent, and attach the kit's "Please Take a Number" sticker to it. Attach the dispenser to the bottom of the tent.

Marvelous Menu

Make a chalkboard menu for your doll's customers!

Food

Make a list of what your doll is going to sell. If you'd like her to sell pastries such as those in the *pâtisserie*, you can list *croissants*, pies, *tartes*, *macarons*, *éclairs*, cakes, and doughnuts. If you'd prefer to sell ice cream, write your doll's favorite flavors on the menu. Or she can sell a variety of breads, like those at the *boulangerie*. Don't forget to write the price of each item.

Drinks

Make a list of the drinks your doll wants to sell, like hot chocolate or orange juice.

Pictures

Remember to draw some pictures on your menu. You can draw ice cream cones, cinnamon rolls, *baguettes*, or cakes. Be as creative as you want.

Chalkboard Writing

Communicate offerings with fanciful and memorable writing.

1. Use a **computer** and **printer** to make the words for the chalkboard. Choose a font and size that will fit the board and be easy to copy.

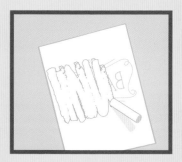

2. Place the printed page over the chalkboard, making sure the words fit. If they do, cover the back of the page with a thick layer of **chalk.**

3. Flip the page so that the chalked side faces the board, and fill in the letters with a **pencil.** The chalk will come off onto the board.

4. Rewrite the letters with chalk or **chalkboard markers.** Embellish the board with 3-D stickers.

Send it in!

Describe your doll's amazing **bakery.**

Send it to:

Baking with Grace Editor

American Girl
8400 Fairway Place
Middleton, WI 53562

Sorry, but photos can't be returned. All comments and suggestions received by American Girl may be used without compensation or acknowledgment.

Here are some other
American Girl books
you might like:

Each sold separately. Find more books at americangirl.com.